Buyer Keywords Profit Formula

Buyer Keywords Profit Formula

Welcome!

First Off, I welcome you and let me start by thanking and congratulating you for purchasing Buyer Keywords Profit Formula.

You have made an **<u>Excellent Decision</u>**

Next I am 100% confident that one you have gone through Buyer Keywords Profit Formula, You will in a better position to judge how powerful this formula is and how easy you can generate big profits using Buyer Keywords.

This method is dead simple and newbies friendly. You don't need to know anything on finding buyer keywords. I will show you step by step how easy the whole system is.

And The best part with you purchase is that I am always there to help you. You can contact me anytime by sending an email at

support@idreesfarooq.com

Also you need to join below group to get any support related to your purchase and also for future update and announcement

https://www.facebook.com/groups/PageOneRankingFormula/

If you would like to promote this product, please contact

Thanks For Your Purchase.
Idrees Farooq
https://www.facebook.com/profile.php?id=100004990669307

TABLE OF CONTENTS

You have taken a great step towards success by picking this course. I have tried my best to make this as easy as possible for you so that you can take action right now.

The whole system is dead simple and laid out in a very simple way for you. Let me summarize every module for you so that you can have an idea how simple it is easy.

In Module 2, I will show how to find the right product. Very straight forward and easy to do. All you need to just follow the instructions and you will good to go.

In Module 3, I will show you what buyer keywords are and how easy you can find them. Remember Buyers Traffic is Money and if you are not selecting right Buyer Keywords to target, I am afraid you will be at Big Fat Zero after your all hard work.

In Module 4, I have shared my own use huge list of Buying Keywords combination that I personally use to find lots of Best Buyer Keywords.

In Module 5, I will discuss about backlinking strategy for Page one Ranking. I will give you my page one ranking strategy for free in this module. You will be surprised so don't skip it.

In Module 6, I will discuss how you can use Buyer Keywords Profit Formula for maximum profits. I have also discussed how you can use Buyer Keywords with SEO, YouTube Marketing and PPC. Don't miss this module.

In Module 7, in the last module, I have added my final thoughts and also conclude Buyer Keywords Profit Formula report for best results.

And Last but not least, Best of Luck. Let's Rock ☺

To Your Success Always

Idrees Farooq
https://www.facebook.com/profile.php?id=100004990669307

Module 1: How to Find the Right Products in Right Niche

Choosing an Affiliate Network

We are going to select Right away an affiliate product that we are going to promote to earn affiliate commission. If you are newbie to SEO and Affiliate Marketing, I would recommend to start with Clickbank Affiliate Network.

There are a lot of other Affiliate Networks including and you can find more about them here. Right now, however, we are going to pick a product from Clickbank Affiliate Network.

Visit Clickbank:

http://www.clickbank.com/. You can Join through the Signup link as per below picture

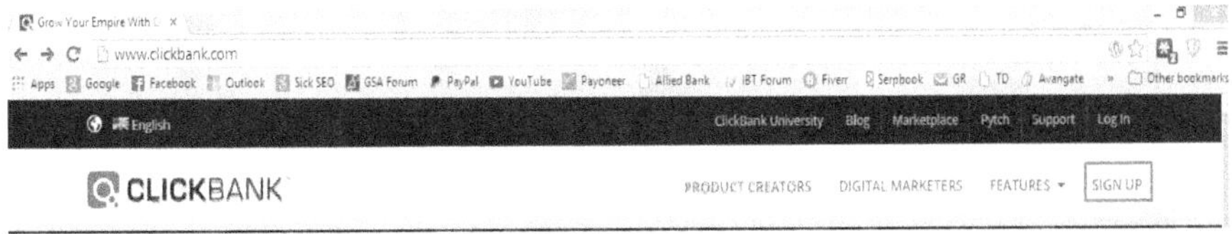

Now you need to fill your information on the next page.

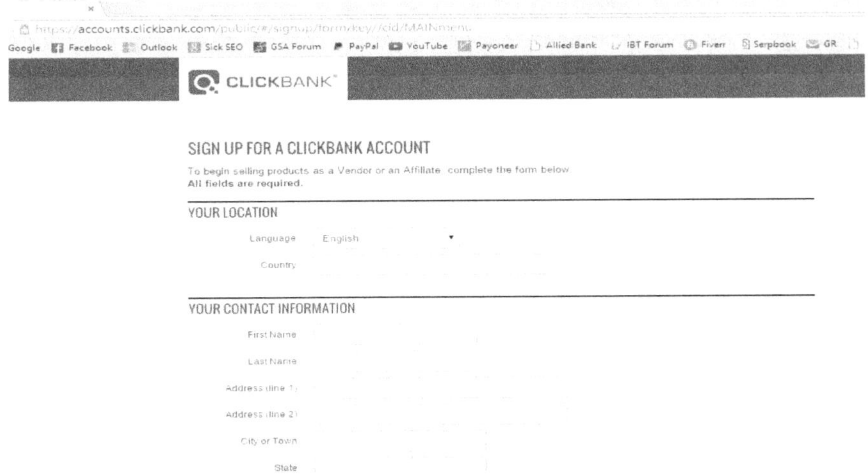

After providing all information and completing the whole process, you will be provided a nickname which is your Affiliate ID.

Clickbank Marketplace

Once you have an Affiliate ID from Clickbank, you can promote products in the Clickbank Marketplace. Now you have affiliates Id, You need to find hot selling products on Clickbank.

Here is a screenshot of Clickbank Marketplace.

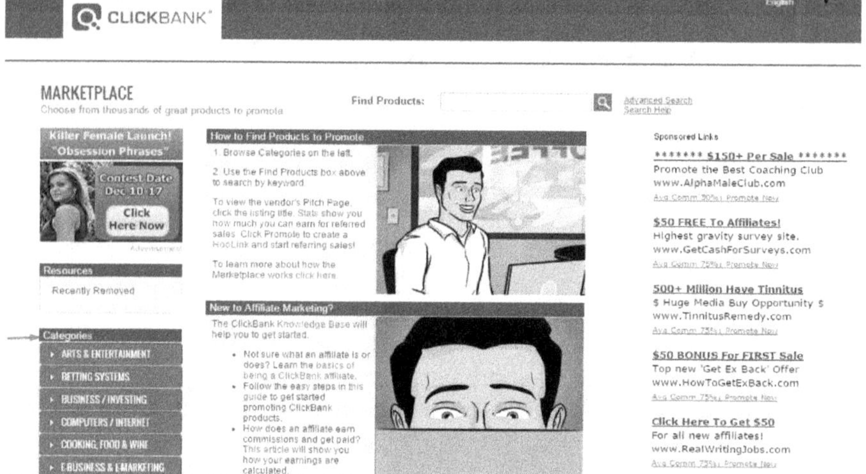

All products from all niches are listed here by Clickbank Vendors. You are now going to pick one product from the categories. Normally these categories are also known as a Niche. So you will select your niche first and then find a hot product in it.

Hot Niches on Clickbank

Being an experienced Affiliate Marketer, I recommend you to just choose a product from one of the below niches or categories

- Green Products
- Health & Fitness
- Home & Garden
- Software & Services

Personally, I normally choose Health & Fitness as I am in the weight loss niche, so most of the products I promote fall under Health & Fitness niche.

Also, don't worry about niche competitiveness, the ranking system I am going to lay down for you in coming modules is so much powerful that you can rank your site in any niche even it is not an affiliate site.

Key Factors of a Right Clickbank Product

Here are 3 key factors of Clickbank for me to find the right product to promote.

- Popularity
- Average Commission per Sale
- Gravity

There are many other factors provided by Clickbank including Refund Rate, Sale Price etc., but you need to give major importance to above 3 factors. These are key factors while choosing a right Clickbank product in the right niche.

On the basis of my criteria, here is my winning product to promote

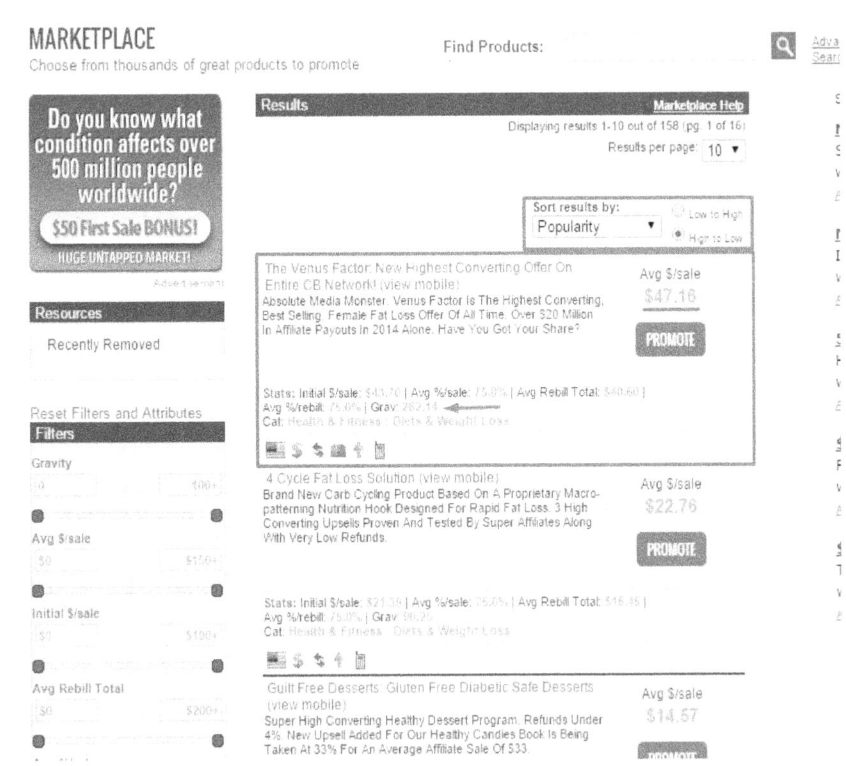

© idreesfarooq.com

I know the power of my Buyer Keywords Profit Formula so I will go with the above product, "The Venus Factor".

Getting Your Hop Link for Clickbank Offer

Now you need to generate your hop link or Affiliate Link which you need to send potential buyers to "The Venus Factor" product sales page. Once somebody will buy this product through your hop link, you will get commission on that sale.

Let's generate Hop Link.

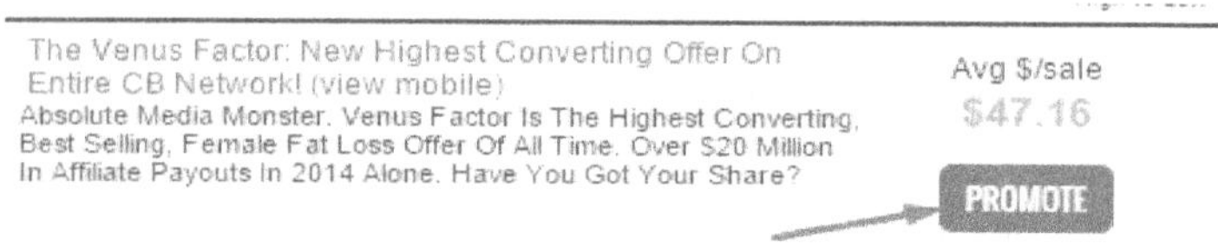

Click on Promote and on the next page you need to put your affiliate id (your account nickname) to get your Clickbank hop link (or Affiliate Link).

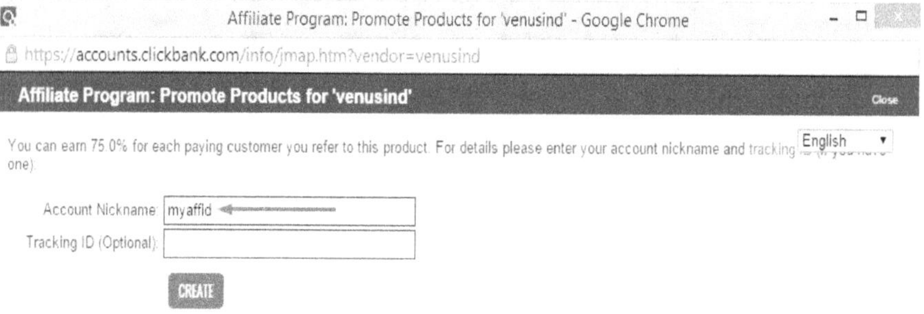

I just put a fake account nickname, however you need to put your real Clickbank nickname to get a correct hop link for you.

If somehow you generate a hop link with a wrong id, you will not able to get commission for any sale you refer to Clickbank.

So be very careful while generating your Clickbank hop link. Now Just click on Create Button and you will get your hop link.

So we are done with our Module1 ☺

We have now selected a hot product which is selling quite well on Clickbank and we have also generated a Clickbank hop link which we used to refer our site visitors to Clickbank. If anyone of them buys "The Venues Factor" product through our affiliate link, we will earn agreed affiliate commission.

Homework for Module 1

- ☐ Visit Clickbank and Create an Account There
- ☐ Select a niche and Find a product to promote.
- ☐ Generate Your Hop Link and Save it in a Text File.

What Keywords are Buyer Keywords?

If you are Into SEO, then this may be the most burning question for you, What Keywords are Buyer Keywords? And the next would be why we need Buyer Keywords?

In next few lines, I am going to show you what actual buyer keywords are and why they are important in your day to day SEO.

Let me define Buyer Keyword first

Buyer Keywords are those keywords which actually provide some urgent solution of a person problem.

For example, if a person is a seeking a solution to lose weight, then a keyword that is actually providing an immediate solution of the problem like a weight loss product name e.g. fat loss factor is a buyer keyword.

Mostly you need to understand that people are looking for 2 types of keywords on the web

1. Informative Keywords
2. Buyer Keywords

"Please make it clear that Informative Keywords are always provided an information about the solution of the problem, whereas Buyer Keywords are always provided immediate Solution of the problem."

- ✓ How To Lose Weight
- ✓ How To Lose Weight Healthy
- ✓ Lose Weight on Food Diet
- ✓ Weight Loss Videos for Women
- ✓ Best Weight Loss Programs

We know these are boring keywords, they have time to spare and they have time to take a look on your site patience.

Examples Buyer Keywords

- ✓ Get Rid of My Belly Fast/3 Day/Overnight/etc.....
- ✓ Fat Burning Device
- ✓ Fat Burning Device Cheap
- ✓ Lose My Belly Fast
- ✓ Fat Loss Factor
- ✓ Buy Fat Loss Factor
- ✓ Where To Buy Fat Loss Factor

So for buying keywords, you see buyers are in rush of need of the product, or intend on getting for the product but might have hesitated about them.

So all is clear now about Buyer Keywords Now ☺

What are Best Buyer Keywords?

You need to understand first that not every Buyer Keyword is the best buyer keyword. You still need to find out the best ones if you have already made a list of Buyer Keywords.

The truth is that one of the best types of "buying intention" keyword is one with the actual product name in it. And I have a very simple formula for you to find best buyer keywords for you.

First Look for Buyer Keyword exactly

"product name"

And then use combination of buying words with product keyword

"product" + discount
"product" + review
"product" + scam
"product" + delivery
 buy "product"

The above mentions examples are the best way to find out your best buying keywords to target.

There are many more Buying Keywords combinations that you can use and then you find out the best buyer keywords for your next affiliate site or YouTube video or PPC campaign.

I have 2 rules when I am finding my best buyer keywords which are:

> For One Affiliate Site I only choose 10 Best Buyer Keywords as it is damn easy to target and get them for free. I will let you know how to find those best buyer keywords for free in this chapter later on.

> I always wanted that those 10 keywords have maximum traffic for that product. There may be some high competition for those keywords, but there would always a competition for those keywords which are actually generating a profit.

This is how I look forward for my Best Buyer Keywords.

Here are my 10 Best Buyer Keywords for my Affiliate Site targeting fat loss factor product of Clickbank.

fat loss factor	5,400
fat loss factor review	1,000
fat loss factor program	720
the fat loss factor	480
fat loss factor free	390
fat loss factor reviews	390
the fat loss factor review	170
fat loss factor book	170
fat loss factor program review	140
fat loss factor by dr. charles livingston	140

See I have my best buyer keywords is product name, keyword and it has also maximum traffic.

This is how I used to find hot and best buyer keywords and in the last section of this chapter how easy I reveal these best buyer keywords for my affiliate sites.

No worries at all, this is all free and you don't need to pay a penny for this, I promise.

Legally Steal Buyer Keywords of Your Competitors

Well, for me this is quite fun. Before starting my own keyword research, I always check how my competitors are targeting Buyer Keywords. This made a lot easier for me to look for only those keywords which actually generating income for my competitor.

I am going to show you how you can legally steal your buyer keywords research in just a few clicks. Remember, you can do it either freeways or through paid tools. Both are good, but my aim is to help you with least amount spent on related stuff other than this book, so I will show you the whole process through freeways.

I only use following 2 tools to find my competitors keywords.

- Google Keyword Planner (Free AdWords Tool)
- Semrush.com (Free Account Only)

I don't use the Google Keyword Planner because of a lot of other hassle and also it does not show competitor's exact ranking in SERP which is a major factor to find his buyer keywords.

I preferred Semrush because it exactly shows those 10 best buyer keywords with ranking position of my competitor.

Let me show you this how I did for my fat loss factor affiliate site. Please note you need to select your product first before you can apply my method of stealing buyer keywords. If you still haven't selected a product, just go back to module 2 and find the right product in the right niche.

"I am assuming for now you have already selected an Affiliate product you are going to promote."

In case you are looking for any advice, you can sent a message here to my facebook Id

https://www.facebook.com/profile.php?id=100004990669307

Here is my step by step method to legally steal my competitor's keywords.

 Put product name "fat loss factor" as a keyword.

You can see I circled **competitor #2** as my main competitor because competitor #1 is the actual Affiliate Site I am promoting. So I am 100% sure that since it is an actual product site, the vendor has not done any sort of keyword research and I cannot find Buyer Keywords. So I go to site #2 as this is an affiliate site.

 Click on main competitor site to steal his keyword search

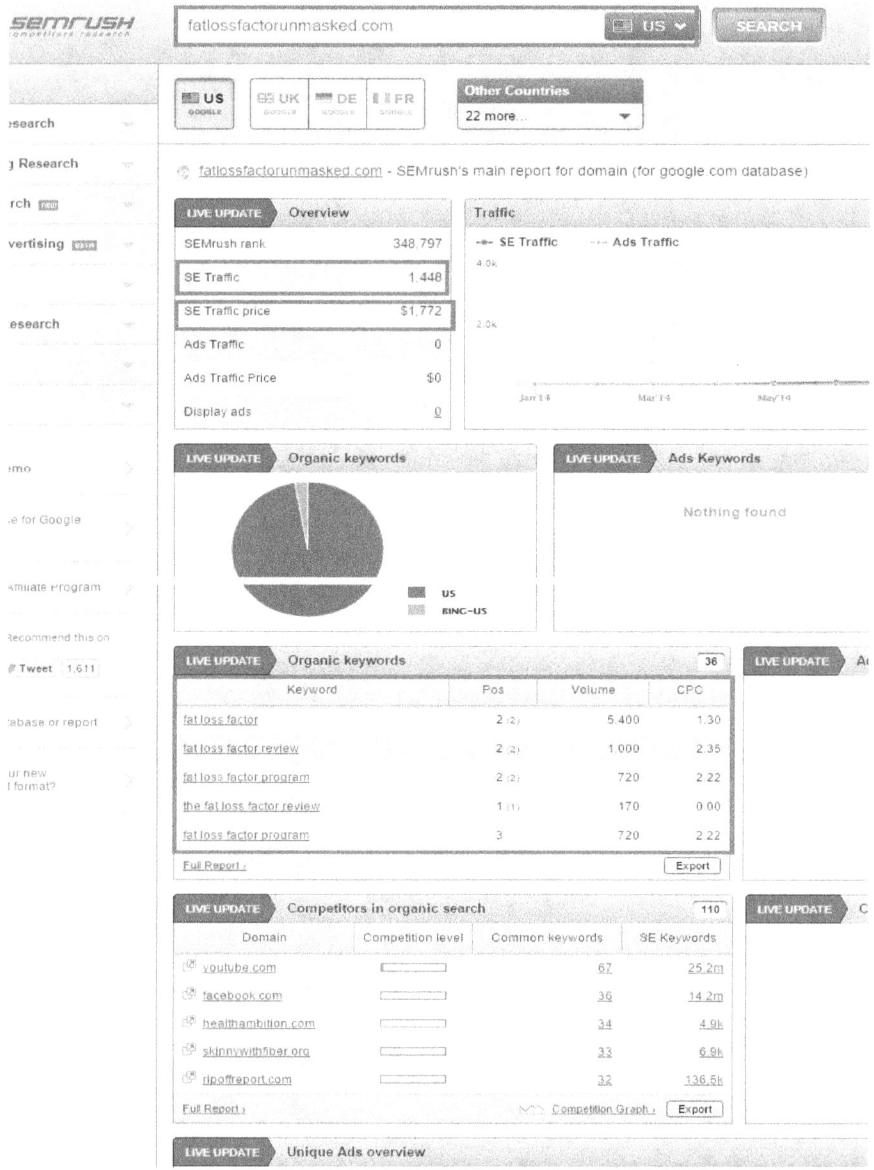

Look how it is. You have all ranked keywords of your competitor in your hand now.

Man, you already did ☺

I mean you have already found high competitive <u>best buyer keyword</u> to target. You just replicate a previous section to find out the Buyer keywords for your affiliate site.

However to get more long tails as an extra add with your buyer keywords, SEO, I would suggest to find out some more long tail keywords. You can use Google Keyword Planner tool to find more keywords or you can use a free tool ubbersuggest to get more suggestions related to your main keyword.

Here is how I find more keyword suggestions using ubbersuggest

Step 1: Enter Product Name

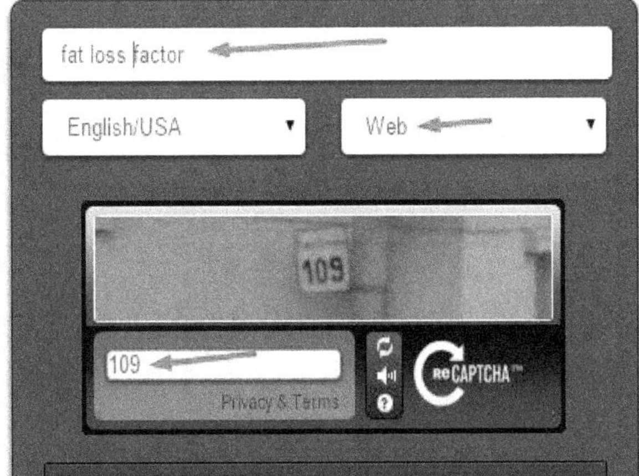

Step 2: **Get Suggestions**

fat loss factor

- fat loss factor
- fat loss factor review
- fat loss factor program
- fat loss factor free
- fat loss factor book
- fat loss factor scam
- fat loss factor pdf
- fat loss factor download
- fat loss factor program free
- fat loss factor cleanse

fat loss factor +

- fat loss factor review
- fat loss factor program
- fat loss factor free
- fat loss factor book
- fat loss factor scam
- fat loss factor pdf
- fat loss factor download
- fat loss factor program free
- fat loss factor cleanse
- fat loss factor program download

fat loss factor + a

- fat loss factor amazon
- fat loss factor affiliate
- fat loss factor affiliate banners

Homework for Module 1

- ☐ Go to Semrush.com and find Competitors Keywords
- ☐ Use Semrush.com to find Best Buyer Keywords
- ☐ Use UbberSuggest. Org to Find Long Tails Keywords

Module4: Huge List of Buying Keywords Combinations

In this module I am providing a huge list of buying keywords combinations that I am personally using to generate Buyer Keywords. I have explained in Module 3 on how to use buying keywords combination to generate profitable buyer keywords. So use my list and generate best buyer keywords.

Here is a huge list of buying keywords combination that I am personally using for my own research. I want to clearly mention that I got most these combinations online from many experts' suggestions while doing research for them. I also add my own buying combinations on the complete list.

Here are Buying Keywords Combinations:

- review
- discount code
- lowest prices
- best prices
- discount
- replacement
- save
- great buy
- code
- sale
- cheapest
- bargain
- compare prices
- shop
- get
- order
- overstock
- best price for
- deal
- codes
- bargain

- promo
- low cost
- discount
- where to find
- sales
- wholesale
- coupon
- special
- cheap
- low priced
- shop
- where to shop for
- offer
- discounts
- buy online
- ratings
- bargains
- bonus
- promotion
- costs
- order online
- best savings for
- prices
- good price for
- cost
- where can i buy
- shop for
- new
- compare
- cheap
- purchase online
- cash back for
- deals
- clearance
- stores
- purchase
- in stock

- ➢ buy
- ➢ in stock
- ➢ coupon code
- ➢ free shipping
- ➢ coupons
- ➢ price
- ➢ store
- ➢ pre order
- ➢ where to buy
- ➢ pre-order
- ➢ lowest price for
- ➢ savings

These are really good buying keywords combinations and you can use them with your product keyword.

That's it for this module.

Homework for Module 5

☐ Use Buying Combination To Find More Buyer Keywords

Module 5: How to Setup Your Money Making Site

Once you have hosted your site, you need to install WordPress on it. WordPress is recommending Content Management System for Page One Ranking Formula System. The best thing is that you don't need to install WordPress manually. Almost every hosting provider will provide you some sort of script solution to install WordPress on your site automatically. Simple Scripts is the one of them and mostly used with cpanel hosting.

To install WordPress you need to login to your cpanel. You can login either directly from your hosting account or by simply typing in your browser bar

- http://www.yoursitename.com/cpanel

Here replace yoursitename.com with your domain id. Once you press enter, you will see panel screen like this.

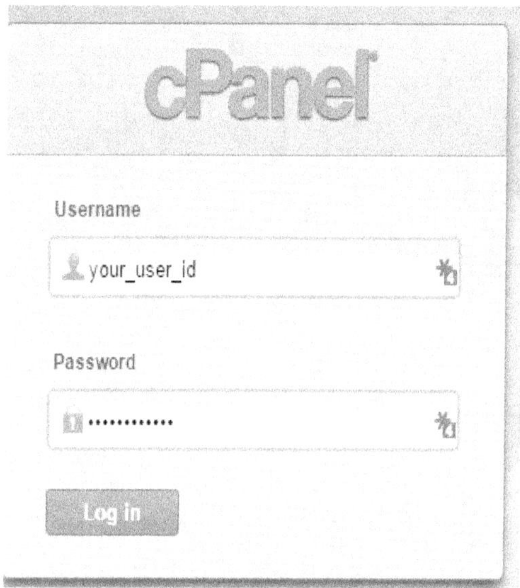

You need to provide your user details to log in to cpanel. Once you log in, you will see cpanel interface like this.

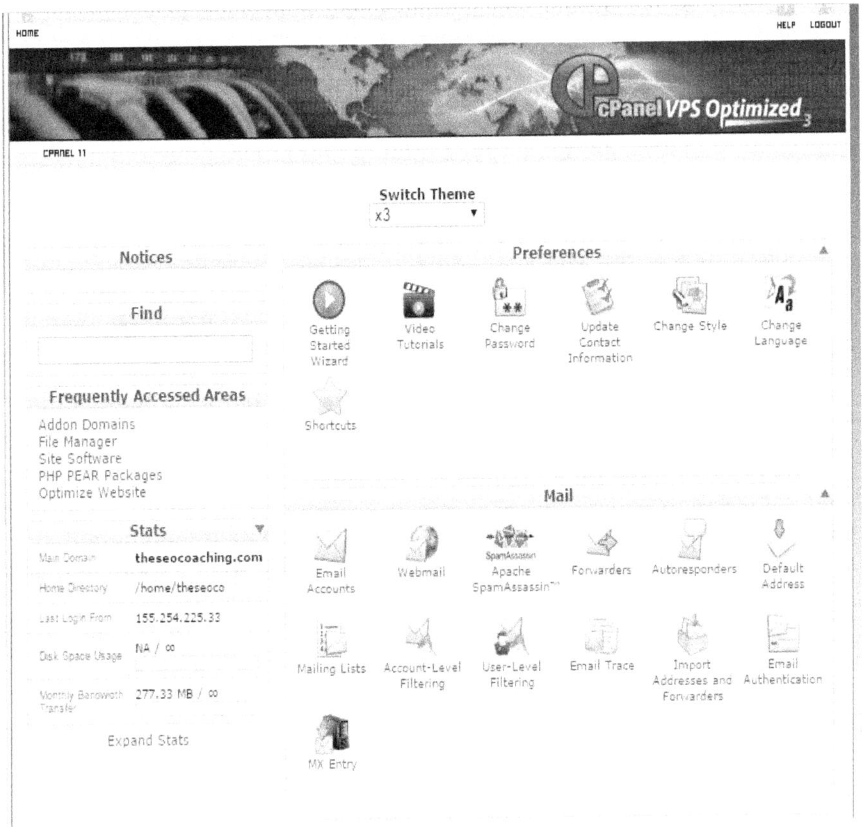

This is not a complete screen shot of cpanel but it's enough for understanding. Scroll down a bit and you will find something like this

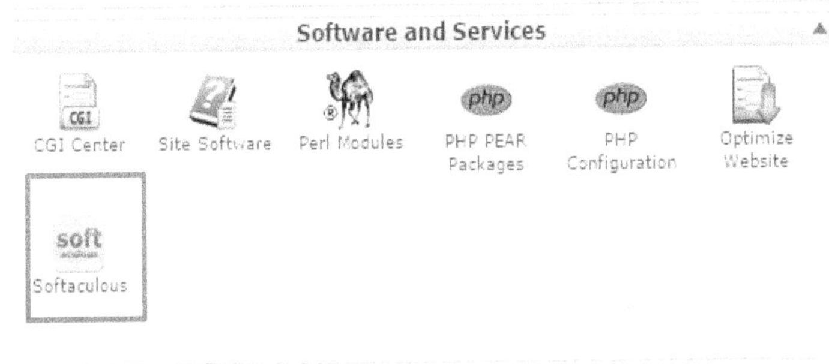

You may find Simple Scripts in your cpanel not like me having Softaculous. However, both are used to do the same, so take it easy. Click on Softaculous Icon and you will see like this.

Top Scripts

Click on WordPress Icon to start installation of WordPress on your domain.

Select your domain in Choose Domain option and then empty in Directory option as shown above.

Just keep other stuff as it is and only add your admin email. One thing you need to change is your WordPress default username Admin to something difficult.

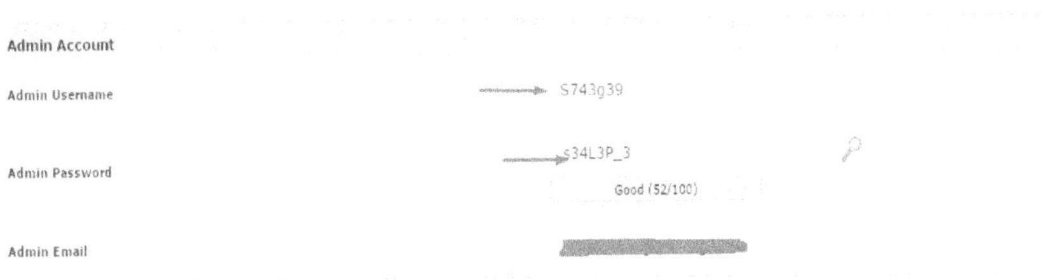

You can see I have change admin username and password to something difficult to understand. This really helps to avid your installation from hacking. Always change your username from Admin to something which is not easy to understand and then setup difficult password. Also add the Admin email you can have access to.

The last thing is you need to put your admin email id and press install button.

This will install WordPress Latest Version on your Domain.

How To Setup Content On Your Site

This is important. You need to understand that we are going to rank our home page of money site against our keyword.

For example, for keyword fat loss factor, I prefer to rank my site http://myfatlossfactorsite.com. We are not going to rank any internal page. Ranking Home page is absolutely important as personally I have seen lots of boost in revenue with those affiliate sites where I have ranked home page of my site.

Here is a complete tutorial how to setup your home page using static page in WordPress

- http://blog.teamtreehouse.com/displaying-a-static-homepage-in-wordpress-treehouse-quick-tip

So you need to do the following things with respect to content.

You must have a 1000 to 1500 product review article which is focused to convince visitors to click on your affiliate link on your home page article. This article is mostly focused to your Target Keyword.

On your home page you need to put a call to action text, affiliate banners and then you can add a sticky widget in sidebar by using a WordPress plugin Q2W3 Fixed widget. It is a free plugin and can be installed from

- https://wordpress.org/plugins/q2w3-fixed-widget/

You need to add at least 5 more blog posts to get more visitors from your longtails anchors once your site is ranked form page one. Don't add all articles at once, just add them on a day after basis.

Install WordPress SEO plugin by Yoast. Activate it and just follow the guidelines provided by WordPress SEO to do on page SEO of your site. Install this plugin from

- https://wordpress.org/plugins/wordpress-seo/

And read the complete tutorial about it from here.

- https://yoast.com/articles/wordpress-seo/

This is How Your Site Should Look Like

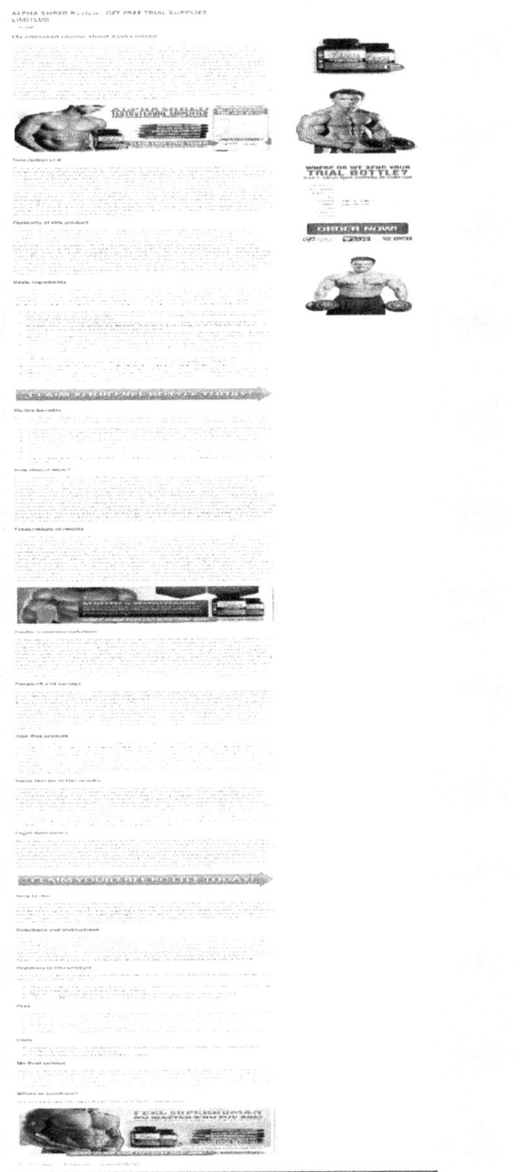

Home Work for Module 5

☐ Install WordPress on Your Domain

☐ Set Up Your Home page with your Product Review Article.

Module 6: Backlinking Strategy for Buyer Keywords

This module is very important for those who are using SEO as their main tool to rank Buyer Keywords. I have also discussed many other ways to make big profits from Buyer Keywords if you don't want to use SEO as your main tool.

You can skip this module if you don't have any interest in SEO but for the rest, I have a complete backlinking strategy plan for you.

Please check Bonus Folder and you will find my Page One Ranking Formula Guide with all resources in it.

Hope you will enjoy with Page One Ranking Formula Guide too. ☺

Homework for Module 5

☐ Check Page One Ranking Formula Guide From Resources

You have your buyer keywords ready and now it is the time to earn big profits from them. You can use Buyer Keywords in many ways to make lots of income for you. Here are a few ways I am using to make big profits and ROI for me.

1) Using Buyer Keywords In SEO
2) Using Buyer Keywords with YouTube
3) Using Buyer Keywords in PPC Campaigns

Using Buyer Keywords in SEO

Being an SEO Expert and Coach from Last few years, I know exactly the importance of Buyer Keywords in my SEO Campaigns.

The SEO Campaigns which are more specifically targeted towards Buyer Keywords are having much better ROI and Profit than those which are targeted to general and informative keywords.

Just like if you are doing IM and List Building, you know the value of the lists either it is a buyer list or a freebie seeker list. The ROI you get from Buyer List is a lot better than freebie seeker lists. The same is the case with Buyer Keywords.

When you are targeting Buyer Keywords in your SEO, the traffic you get to your affiliate site is already having buying mindset. You don't need to do much to make affiliate sales for the products you are promoting.

In my personal experience with some weight loss affiliate sites, I observed that I normally made one affiliate sale from 15 to 20 visitors to my site. Remember, we don't need huge traffic to earn good from our affiliate sites while targeting them with Buyer Keywords. A little traffic can bring a good number of sales and profit.

I can easily say with 100 visitors daily while targeting with Buyer Keywords, $100 a day is achievable if your affiliate commission per sale is more than $30 which is quite normal in weight loss product.

So go ahead and try adding Buyer Keywords in your SEO Campaigns and make big profit.

Using Buyer Keywords with YouTube

If you are a video marketer, creating affiliate videos while targeting Buyer Keywords can add great profit.

I have personal experience of ranking YouTube Affiliate Video not only Page One on Google but also on YouTube. I always able to generate lots of sales and leads doing this way.

Here is great tips for video marketers that I personally use for me.

> Always Target Buyer Keywords in Video Title

> Don't link your video directly to your Affiliate Link. Send all Video traffic to Your Affiliate Site which will act as landing page. This works a lot better and you can capture leads also to target them later with email marketing.

> Try to rank your video on Google Page one. That will bring a lot more traffic that if you try to rank it on YouTube only. I have personally experienced that if my Video is ranked on Google, it also ranked on YouTube. Test, Test and Test, the only way to succeed.

If you are doing PPC and specially using Adwords or Bing Ads, you need to make sure that your keywords must be relevant. The relevancy of your keywords depends on your niche. However, adding Buyer Keywords to your PPC Campaigns can result in big profits for you.

I am personally using Bing Ads for my PPC and I can ensure you that I have great results with it. I am targeting my affiliate sites with mostly Buyer Keyword and the results are awesome.

Keep in mind the overall goal while using PPC as your traffic tool is to drive paid traffic to your product review site where your affiliate links are placed. If your Ads perform at their maximum potential using Buyer Keywords, You can generate a lot of money in short time.

However, you need to put lots of tweaking before making big money through PPC. I personally recommend a great PPC training, PPC **Kraze** where Vincent provided 77 pages in depth training about PPC.

So Best of Luck with your PPC Campaigns using Buyer Keywords. Don't forget to let me know your results.

Homework for Module 6

- ☐ Find Buyer Keywords and Add Them to Your SEO
- ☐ Create YouTube Video using Buyer Keywords
- ☐ Setup PPC Campaign with Buyer Keywords

Module 7: Conclusion and Final Thoughts

Congratulations on completing Buyer Keywords Profit Formula. You actually done a great job and learned the most important stuff, i.e. Finding Best Buyer Keywords and Earning Big Profits from them.

To be a successful with Your Buyer Keywords Research, I would like to give 3 point formula

1) Finalize Best Buyer Keywords For Your SEO, YouTube Video or PCC Campaigns

2) Stick with It. Don't let your focus away from your set target.

3) Work Hard and Make Big Profits and ROI

I always asked to my students that there is no magic stuff like Push Button formula to get rich quick. You still need to do Work Hard and Hard till you achieve your set goals.

If you are expecting that you will start making thousands of dollars overnight, then I'm afraid none of my "Formula" product series can help you.

However, I am back my products with my 100% Guarantee that If you apply my method that I teach you in them with their complete spirit and work hard, you will get results. Just give some time or a set period of 3 months and you will see a huge boost in your income and online business.

You and Only You are the biggest factor for your success in your business and achieving your goals. And you can definitely do it.

Just believe on words "YES I CAN"

Please don't hesitate to contact with me for any help regarding my both products

Page One Ranking Formula

Buyer Keywords Profit Formula

And also anything related to Online Business. I will be much happier to help you to your success. I have made tone of money online and I want same Financial Freedom for you too.

So if you have a question for me, ask me. Just submit a support email

support@idreesfarooq.com

or sent me a message here at facebook

https://www.facebook.com/profile.php?id=100004990669307

And I will respond you in least possible time with my take on your question.

You can also provide your feedback on this product and give suggestions to improve it. I will be happy to add those suggestions in the upcoming version and update of this product if any.

Looking forward to hear from you. Best of Luck.

<u>Thank You for Purchasing Byer Keywords Profit Formula!</u>

Thanks

Idreesfarooq